LILAC V

Poems
by
Martyn Hesford

Martyn Hesford is a BAFTA-nominated writer. His film screenplays include FANTABULOSA! starring Michael Sheen, and MRS LOWRY AND SON starring Vanessa Redgrave and Timothy Spall.

LILAC WHITE is Martyn Hesford's first collection of poetry.

for

my friend

Penelope Patrick

1

we waved
our wands
and slowly
your world
started
to disappear.

can you feel it?
your power
is going.

Beauty
is soaring
above the Beast.

2

a lilac hat
a lilac coat
a lilac shirt

his hair
is long

his lips
are red

there are
moths

white and black

pinned
to his
skin

he lowers
his eyelids
and sees
no one

only me

he is pinned
to me

a butterfly

I keep
under glass.

3

is this
the place?

yes

this is
the place

it happened
here

listen

can you
see?

hear

the tiny mementoes

the shapes

the
coloured glass
trinkets

the people

tie
them

to

the tree

tinkle

tinkle

in memory
of

the murdered boy

the tree
of colours

the glint

the white

the red

blue

sparkle

twinkle
twinkle

under
moon and star

here is

the sentimental

tinkle

twinkle

the preservation

of

their

glass tears.

4

blue is smudged
into a chair

white is left
on a door knob

the whispering
of
the stars

the sighs
of
the moon

the sun
splutters and hisses

a deep sea rumbles

the whizzing of the world

like a spinning top

the colours
submerge

they mix
into one

the sound
becomes a note

the invisible

the visible

the silence

the stillness

the presence

the magic

the mystical

all are

your cloak

your crown

in
the throne room

of silver

secrets.

5

I hold
a rainbow

in my pocket

a little rainbow
that survived

a holocaust

rainbows
once upon a time

were everywhere

until they
were hidden

locked away
(by them)

murdered

one
by
one
by
one

murdered

explained away

(by them)

quietly
quietly

they died.

(in a hush).

6

they were stolen

the old magic spells

locked away.

the men
of knowledge
tried to
explain
everything

away.

didn't they know?

there is no
answer.

no answer
to anything.

nothing
is final.

finished

ended.

one life
leads
to another.

a question
is the same

leading
to
the other.

then
another
and
another.

all is
in the labyrinth

the egyptians
knew this

the pagans
knew this

the gypsies
knew this
too

the magicians
the mystics
the martyrs
the messiahs
of old

the seers
they knew

oh yes

they did

know

nothing is new
here

it's time
to remember

what

the world
has forgotten

listen
and you
will
hear it

under
every stone
and rock

under
a boulder

the mountains

listen to
their whispers

insects are speaking

telling
us

what we
really
are

where
we came from

where
we are
going

there is nothing
more to know
than this

we are
all

the same

this moment
here

a piece
of dust.

slowly
turning

slowly
twirling

slowly
swirling

the one

the same

little spec.

stardust.

7

when
you walk
down
the street

you
look like
any
other
boy

but
I can see
the difference

a crown
hovers
over
your blond head

a crown
of blood

the band
of the crown
drips

red

nobody can
see

you

cannot

see

is it a symbol?

a dream?

what
is your reason

for being

here?

I know
the world
will murder you

I have
been here
before

they will
let

you

wear
the crown

when

you

are

dead

they will call

you

their
holy one

I can
see

you

now

a child

a boy

with tears
in his eyes

the smile
of innocence

walking
down
the street

with
a thousand others

all
falling
(behind you).

8

broken

white

heart glass
felt

in
red

forever.

the little
sailing boat

floats
on the blue.

past

the purple
Island.

there is
a mauve
halo

invisible
to all.

in

this

picture.

I can see it.

the luminous

the two

white pure
fasting angels
sitting

on
the silver tree

like chalk.

all is
a fragile

a purity.

nothing
is dead here.

the little
red fruit

the winter
red berry

the blood

the food

of
the little saint

feeds him.

while

the three

white and blue

stars

appear
inside

the black.

on
the horizon

all is
good.

broken
never.

the peace

is shining

in
the little

child's

golden crown.

the spring

a white
flower

here

comes.
again.

forever.

never gone.

the wound

crimson cracked

melts

into
the snow.

a gentle hush
is the movement of wings.

the silence.

a prayer.

all is heard
today

yesterday

and
tomorrow.

all is
healed.

all is
forgiven.

moment after moment after moment.

the sigh

the sigh

the sigh.

9

you stand
in the redness

up to your knees

you wear
a purple
white lily

fixed
onto
your skin

I can see

thorns.

you are
looking
at me
again

with

half a smile

you wait

patiently

you stand
in the corner

of my father's
house

you

with a broken
tooth

you never speak
ever

just watch.

will we

ever

speak?

I wonder

what will you say
to me?

I wonder.

I know you watch
me
night and day

dressing

undressing

are you
to be

my lover?

the stealer

of

innocence.

(my)

innocence.

this

lonely boy's desire
pricked.

10

the glass cut my hand.

sharp.

then
I noticed
him

wearing

a tall
transparent
crown

he didn't
speak

not a word

his breathing
felt
close

warm

he holds
out his hand

and romance
blossoms

in

the first

gesture

there is something
eternal here

there is life
and death.

we kissed

breathing life.

life into life.

life into
our death.

knowing
loneliness

together

always

beside

the midnight tree

staring

upwards

beckoning

the golden
comet

we bathe
in light.

11

flowers tied

cut.

always

feel

lonely.

they die
to be

free.

again the whiteness. the beautiful falling snow. the dream of a bride dancing in the rain. to begin again. hope is the innocent smile. we will kiss. the light. one day. the sun. the dance on the water. burning forever and forever is the flare. "Oh" is the sigh. at first the scream. then. the dissolve. into nothing. the end alone. yet. not alone. always. the light. a beginning. the one winter star.

within.

13

I am
the first and last kiss

see

the tree
on the hill

all is magnificent

all is

a small
miracle.

light
bright
sight
white

can you
see it

feel it

the crispness

of the
crystal

(clear)

the
light
bright
sight

the moment
white

(morning).

I can.

the clarity
of (today)

the
light
bright
white

breaking

fragment

of tomorrow.

the sigh
the sight

the sparkle

the brightness
blinding

binding

yesterday.

the essence

the pain

the sorrow

the smile

of

each swirling particle.

now

the spirit.

the world

a breath.

the blue white
butterfly.

in a single tear

the fear.

in

a tiny white pearl

a little laugh.

small

the warmth.

all that
is wished for.

a prayer

the spell

is a God

given

gift.

14

I am cold.

my heart is broken

but not
yet

frozen.

there is star dust
on my fingers

and moon dust
in my lungs

the river is almost silent
as it flows

but not
quiet

yet.

freesia
violets
mimosa
primroses

the first
and last

flowers

I put onto your grave

here
I made

the fear

laugh.

nothing
here

need
be

explained

nor taken

away.

we know
that.

all
is innocence.

all
is a radiance.

a snowflake

melting

into my hair.

the
blinding

bright light

of
God's
white flare.

the memory.

a life

my brother

all here

is

still.

you.

15

a thousand
tiny stained glass windows
broken
into fragments
a thousand years
of prayers heard
the sorrow
the joy
the birth the death
the singing
held in the strength
of lead veins

forever
is their
presence

a thousand tiny glass windows
broken
into fragments

splinters
found
held

become
your wings.

16

I shake

the branches

(the sentimental tree)

I let
the flowers
fall

I stamp
in anger

into the mud

from
a seed

a tree
a true feeling

a flower

will

grow.

lilac

white.

17

the earth
and
the moon

the night long star

I am
completely
alone
here

I can see
my fingers

my arms
my legs

feet
nipples
toes

every nude stitch.

I stand
here
holding
my arms
upwards

stretching
breathing

a boy
in the night.

I walk
through
the swish tickle
of grass

I look
into the stream

I see
myself

first
time
ever

a boy

in the black
pitch
night dark
earth

in God

and
nobody
told
me

and
nobody
said

I could
come
here

do this

in God

nobody

said I
could come

here

clean

and enter

the silence

the dark

the silver

the grace

the sex

in nature

every nude stitch.

of God.

18

mirrors.

everything covered
in snow

held in my hand.

you

I remember
the sparkle.

gleaming.

the clean
and pure.

the crystal
snowflake

air.

swirling like water

a glass dome

a glass world

a glass man

our world

the liquid
sound of birds.

19

I have
watched

all

for sixty years

and
i still

believe

in
white
orchids

the white lily

the lilac white

and

the odd

beautiful

black

purple

tattoo.

to hide

many

a

bruise.

20

the soft sound
of rain
on a glass
pane
always
gives me
tears
inside

a lost memory

somewhere
I love.

21

all
I wanted
was
a dog
to call
my own.

a thing to love.

I have trapped
myself

in the dark
in the house

I have closed
every white
wooden shutter
to the world

I can still hear the sea shouting

I am locked
away

in the house

a thousand
safe
rooms

I'm here

with you

and
that's all
that
matters.

I am locked away in the house.

tied up
tied together

out of sight
silent

safe.

22

there is perfume waiting
on a shelf
waiting
to be
opened.

there is light
reflected
in a mirror

waiting
to be

seen.

the room is summer

the rustle of
silk

the breeze

the echo of a piano

all is beautiful
here
a perfection

crisp

clean

in black and white.

along the corridor a wife sews

her children play

the husband and the lover

play their games
of tangled ropes

the perfume
the light
the mirror

the gash
the bite

the slow slow

seeping of red

this house
had a secret.

undiscovered.

the cutting away of white
the sipping the drinking

the warm warm brandy

the falling white petal

the piercing of skin

the blood and the flesh

the worship
a reflection the desire his love

her cold life.

the seed the growth the flower

the perfume waiting

on a shelf
to be opened

inhaled

skin on skin

the kiss after kiss after kiss

the taste

mouth on mouth
stitch after stitch

now
all gone.

this happening
of a summer.

the guilt
of never knowing
or saying

I love you.

the blossoms
shielded it all

but the little wasp
still
stings.

23

I need

to run

sometimes.

rip

the sky
open

taste the fear

I need to jump

I need to fall

laugh

cut myself

love myself

close my eyes

see

the silver world

eat
the lilac flower

and

breathe.

24

white lilac

lilac white

is the movement

the tremulous

on the blue

the beauty of form.

25

the glamour
is coming.

the victorian
ghosts
are being
hung back
into their wardrobes.

the new apparitions
are rising.

do not be angry
do not be afraid.

it has been
one way

your way

for a very long time.

share
and share
alike
my genderless
lipstick

kiss me.

honey
honey

kiss me.

I forgive you.
I love you.
will you

love

me?

ever.

I am your eye (s)
shadow.

Your

lilac

white

sparkle

star

flower.

Printed in Great Britain
by Amazon